Praise for *L*

M000234044

Let There Be Light does exac supposed to these days: it takes its subject seriously. Structured in a reverse sequencing of the Book of Genesis (ending on the First Day with a marvelous, bold sequence that will literally leave you in the dark), *Let There Be Light* is not a God book, at least not in the usual way. It is a book deeply spiritual, but its spirit derives from a commitment to the terrestrial and a careful attention to why the terrestrial matters. ~Nick Twemlow

Did we need a *Memento*-style reverse and idiosyncratic re-telling of the Biblical creation story? No. But does Nick Courtright's *Let There Be Light* make us glad we have one now anyway? Yes. ~Kathleen Rooney

Nick Courtright's *Let There Be Light* sings of a place where creation and destruction exist as one, discovering beauty and possibility even in the darkest and most puzzling corners of the world. ~Adam Clay

The heady, ambitious poems in *Let There Be Light* pan a wide-angle lens over all creation, taking on weighty questions about the origin and meaning of life on Earth. Like Adam, Courtright is calling roll in a world where there are no coincidences, and nothing is the same after its naming. ~Rebecca Hazelton

Nick Courtright's excellent second collection, which chronicles the seven days of creation in reverse order, dismantles what can be said and what can be known, leading us backward into a stunning, rectangular darkness. ~Allison Benis White

Let There Be Light is like a model of the solar system where every planet is the sun, an ecosystem where bear and prophet regard the universe and all its mysteries with equal awe. ~Mary Biddinger

What a feat! You can walk backwards and forwards along these poems and not find death. ~Emily Kendal Frey

Praise for *Punchline*

With its one-two of exuberant wit and vigorous philosophical inquiry, Nick Courtright's *Punchline* is nothing short of a knockout. ~Timothy Donnelly

Between the infinity of the universe and the futility of small matters, along with the prophet and the fatalist, *Punchline* travels. It's a tightrope performance Nick Courtright is embarking on here, knowing full well that these necessary turns to the large abstractions of "enlightenment" and the "apse of consciousness" are hanging threadbare above us, and at any moment all our understanding could be "revised by pamphlets fallen / from the sky, or by Adobe Photoshop." These are fundamental, open questions, and they anchor a wonderful book. ~John Gallaher

By turns elliptical and aphoristic, macrocosmic and microcosmic, timeless and contemporary, *Punchline* is not a book of poems for those who merely want to be diverted or amused; this work is for readers who consider poetry the natural sibling of philosophy. Nick Courtright's finely-distilled poems mine the frustrating unknowableness of the world, and celebrate its exhilarating mystery with elegance, compassion, and imagination. ~Nicky Beer

Nick Courtright

GOLD Wake Press

Boston, Massachusetts

L
E
T

THERE

B

E

LIGHT

CONTENTS

for Alice and Marvin

THE SEVENTH DAY

Thus the heavens and the earth were finished, and all the host
of them. And God blessed the seventh day, and sanctified it:
because that in it he had rested from all his work which God
created and made.

POLITIC

The internet is a pile of transmissions, like much else.

And anger is a handbasket full of sound
and sweet notes
left on the doorstep. Last year

more than four million American babies were born

and there's not too much that that can mean.

A dream watches other dreams
like an animal
fighting itself
within a burlap sack. Many minutes pass,

and marvelous springtime eyes its own predictable mess
as new life trembles beneath the wind.

Meanwhile, a religion found only on mountaintops

composes songs for the future, as you climb stairs
climbed by the past.

Therefore, foreign policy is yet another irony,

and leafing through a photo album is history and architecture:

in a photograph, what replaces memory
is a pose

that does not change, regardless of whether the picture

is held close to the face, like this,

or very far from the face, like this.

THE YOUTH

Late at night, a shadow becomes its own
life alive on the wall or curtain, and when it moves

a piece of everywhere
moves with it. Is that okay?

In this world, it is good sometimes to be afraid.

And in this telling
of the story, some of the fish went to waste.
They lay in heaps, the spectacle complete.

Every life
has its own light, and the sayings of confident men
don't make trees

subject to interpretation. They flash and bob
as they please. Is that okay?

Still, we are still

here. Like ghosts in love

with the living, we listen but find it difficult to speak.

TYRANNOSAURUS

The caves in which we live our days are not real
but the bear inside them is.

That's what is real: the bear.

To believe this is to pull out the tablecloth
from under Thanksgiving dinner and say ta-da!

Maybe the food is on the floor, maybe it's all ruined.

Maybe you did that on purpose, sprung the birds

from their cages to watch them fly around the dining room,
their little beaks like darts.

Or maybe you say ta-da!

and everything on the table is still, everyone is
astonished by your charm and the quickness of your hands.

Lift them in the air and pat yourself on the back, for years—
your bear could be erased

but it's too much to believe you won't last forever,
or that you will.
See? You can't trust the cave.

Now, play dead.

Then they won't see you, they can't see you
if you aren't moving. But we aren't all dinosaurs.

LOST ON THE PLANET EARTH

When we go missing, we can blame

the search team, the rescue squad, the fleet of helicopters
competing with the calls of wild birds.

We can blame the earthworms

moving the land beneath us, the day
both too long and not long enough,

and the fact that, in these new bodies, we have
only so much time.

We can fault the immensity of the galaxy, the smallness
of the human soul,
the clouds

which have their way with the light of the sun

as it is brought across the backs of whales, or harpooned
across the face
of the empty moon, deep

in the black soup of night.

When we go missing, we can heave our blame
into the wind

of our grandparents' grief and love

which mirrored
the unspeakable desire

of the first two cells

who came together
in the petri dish of an early ocean.
We could even blame America, the outspoken, and the rich.

Or we could take credit
for our missing,
for how we wandered from where we were born,

that the maps we chose were outdated, all the roads long gone
or curiously mismarked,

that each step we took into the plain, or into the plan
was in fact into the forest,

where what was watching us
was watching itself.

And maybe, when we are finally found

our finders too will have become lost,
and will have discovered not only us, but themselves.

THE HUMAN EXPERIENCE

But what is its rationale? See, earth has nothing to do
with it. Neither does the sun,

but mostly Venus
has nothing to do with it, being so small

and marble.

It'll be the same old story, story, story, told
by someone close to death
and that someone

could be anyone, we are all in our own way
so very close.

In just a few short minutes a lunar eclipse will reveal itself.

From a mere two hundred twenty-one
thousand miles from earth

the missing slice of moon appears almost perfect,

as if it were a perfect bite made by a perfect, godly mouth.

This bite mark may conjure

a memory of apples,
which could easily
lead to Eden, and to depravity

and desire and urges and lust, and straight

back to Venus,
the romantic image of utter, absolute beauty.

But what is not absolute beauty? Let's be serious.

THE SIXTH DAY

So God created man in his own image, in the image of God created he him; male and female created he them. And God blessed them, and God said unto them, Be fruitful, and multiply, and replenish the earth, and subdue it: and have dominion over the fish of the sea, and over the fowl of the air, and over every living thing that moveth upon the earth.

PARABLE

Once upon a time there was a rich man who sat down for a meal with the devil.

They ate lamb and drank wine and ignored such things' attendant cries.

The rich man wanted more, that is why he was with the devil—people do not invite the devil to dinner unless they want. That is the way of such negotiations.

So the rich man says I want three wishes.

And the devil says, who am I? I am no genie. You get one request so make it good.

The rich man takes another sip of wine. Then I wish for an immortal life with endless material bounty.

The devil takes another bite of meat. That is two wishes, but how about this: I grant your wishes, so long as you accept one condition.

Yes, then, says the rich man.

I assumed you would agree, and that is good. Here is what I want from you: you will have all you desire, an immortal life of incalculable wealth, but you will forever after have a small, sharp rock in your shoe.

17

And so it was.

Now imagine that man with his endless life and goods, and with the rock in his shoe. Got that? Now imagine the life of the rock.

HOLIDAY

Ireland of the post-glaciers
never was home
to snakes, so St. Patrick had little work

to do. The better world was already on
its way, the wrinkles in the hands
of anyone's great grandfather no cause

for worry. That's how things were—childhood
moved across the carpet
with the grace of a bat,

which means "no grace." What is possible
is that the bat was offended
by such judgments, that the woman upstairs

pounding about the floor
in tune to her workout video
is *this close* to God. I believe that,

why not? Sillier things have caused enlightenment,
the palm of a man
on the forehead of another, the heat

of holy water upon the nape
of a neck, the father of a daughter realizing
what he cannot control...

MEDITATION ON THE BEAR
FINDING HIMSELF

I do not know what to make of the bear
who eats and does not watch

the night fall into its curtains. He may or may not be snow

as it breaks beneath his feet, or the feet themselves.

Certainly he is the branches which moan in the wind. Listen.
They have stories to tell

but if no one is there to hear them…

We don't have to be carried away
by our ships and our trains. They are seams in the dress
named landscape. Or they are wounds which cannot heal—

once upon a time the monster of Frankenstein
could have wandered here.

It's not in the book, or the movies,
but he and the bear crossed paths, like two ships…

How often did the bear growl, or roar?
In dreams, as often as he remembers his mother.

—Now imagine him in his crib, as he is a cub.

Imagine him near the river, as he kills what he can.

Imagine him eyeing his claws, wondering what have I done.

I have done this, he could say. I have provided this meal.

NEAR-DEATH EXPERIENCE

Sometimes the pews of a church last hundreds of years.

People sit on them
and grow tired, and they do this until they need waking up.

When they wake
we whisper

what is it like to live forever?

THE CIRCUIT

They say now everything is connected,

the thin green vein on the ear's back, the wires running
beneath your sheet of skin,

the bone-white bones
on which the rest of things hang, shivering—

I saw the speeding car last night and the cat, where they met.

On occasion, the need for trembling
leaves, and returns.

And a crown of moon
wears the cricketing mid-autumn trees

straight through to their ripe, wooden centers—

if everything is connected,
about dying, how can we not feel better than we do?

This is all I remember: the fullness

of cooling asphalt beneath my shoeless feet, the twilight buzz of the streetlamp, and the lifting of the limp,

breathless dead, to be cradled, very gone, and very real.

A BRIEF ESSAY ON SAMENESS

To know the news of one day
is to know the news of any day.

When Thoreau implied this

he sounded, as he often did, like a magnificent grump,
yet while the specifics change, and can dramatically,
the themes remain the same—

tragedy, speculation, astonishment, intrigue,
voyeurism, accomplishment,
amusement, profit, and sometimes resolution—while all

the smoke in the air is air

and the ones you love

sleep in peace in their beds, minutes reach out
like rail lines...

To a philosopher, all news, as it is called, is gossip.

Never mind the news. Maybe we're getting old, or maybe
we already were.

•

Idea: curiosity is a kind of lust.

It is a shape of beauty formed from dirt: it is why an animal
does not meet next year, but goes on

without its body.

The way it is is as it has always been.
But as Hume

asserts, we cannot argue tomorrow will be the same as today
based on knowledge of yesterday,

and we mustn't assume

our experience will remain as it presently is
forever.
It could change spontaneously and without warning.

Knowing this, the infant
is immune to boredom, for all

she sees is new. Why, then, are the rest of us different,

for when do we see
what truly
we have seen before?

•

Like stepping into the same river twice, many paradoxes
resolve

with a little clarification
of definition:

the ship of Theseus, conveyor

of the slayer of the Minotaur, so revered
Athens aimed to preserve it, and whose wooden panels

were replaced as they ruined, illustrates this fact:

was the ship truly that of Theseus, even after in its entirety
it had been, plank by plank, transformed?

Idea: idea

remains long after the physical has been

corrupted, or bettered. *Idea:* the ship wholly
will always be, for eternity, a symbol of courage, and of lust.

Idea: even this can be wrecked, or bettered. *The night sky.*

•

Why? Because apples were tributes to the seasons,

carrots were tributes to the sun,

almonds were tributes to the eyes of angels,

and leaves were tributes to every leaf. *But who left those apples
long past their brilliance*

on this land? Who, in doing so, compromised all the world's tributes?

From then on
the apple came to represent

ruin, destruction, the corruption

of God's tribute to himself, woman,
man, innocence, sensibility, and making

this earth not beauty

for forgetting, but ugliness to remember. And because of
this,

this week, our very first week, has been
the longest week of all.

THE FIFTH DAY

And God created great whales, and every living creature that moveth, which the waters brought forth abundantly, after their kind, and every winged fowl after his kind: and God saw that it was good. And God blessed them, saying, Be fruitful, and multiply, and fill the waters in the seas, and let fowl multiply in the earth.

31

THE DEEP

A phone rings unanswered into the vast universe.

The ring between men and women
and the children they share

rings endlessly into the endless universe.

And in dreams the ring is absorbed
by suns and the careless tails of comets, it is redirected

by dark energy, it is loved
by dark energy.

But it's already too late. It's time to wake.

Please, please eternity, leave your message—
there's plenty of room
to crawl from the nest.

Caller, I hear you, I hear your voice
beloved by honey, danced upon by bees. I fold into it.

So like the red canyon between a syllable's beginning
and its conclusion,

or like the knotted mass of thought
in the knee
of a thousand-year-old tortoise, perfect

is the empty space in which the tortoise calls out, *I am
your father*

and if you hurled me into the sea

*I'd surely perish, and if you climbed onto my shell
I'd carry you, questionlessly.*

SONNET FOR THE AIRBORNE

There is no hurry but even hawks

harbor radiance. Their mothers fed them

graciously, that charity of mothers, every mother, regardless
of what dreams have been tangled in the wreckage.

Don't forget this or failure will find you,

or the hawk will find you. When you sleep
it will say
I am home, this is my home.

You can go into the darkness
too many drinks later, to find that everything you do is fine.

You can ask a stranger for money. You can make a habit of it.

Who knows whose money it is, anyway,
or if we are all two birds making love in the rain—it is

all our money, and we are alive. Ghosts cannot change us.

TRAVELOGUE

The map was folded again and again, each time
just a little differently

until your hometown on the crease
was white with folding.

It was as if your childhood
had been taken away,

as if your adolescence were just a field of white,
your birth in the folding

only an absence of color, so many times
spread over the dashboard in confusion—

memories were the sky you'd drive into
for twenty thousand hours

to come out on Mars, among the red rocks
where all the wishes you had or were to have

were on the map—would this road dead end,
would this dusty path continue on forever?

Imagine your life, its rollings over and turns
of phrase, as a kind of driving through

all our maps' white spaces, the sun in the rearview—
would you like a cup of tea upon your arrival?

I wanted two doves, two mourning doves
to wake me, I wanted to say

joy   *joy*
but the tea was cold by the time I found my way.

THE NIGHTLY NEWS

Half the world is lost in the canyon,

half of the market
and of the lamplight, and half the raspy voices of children

who eat stones for breakfast. Half the world is lost.

Do not be worried. It was always lost.

Italy, Mongolia, Zaire lost to ambition and to the canyon.
Brazil lost to water, America to the whales.

Behind the waterfall, a face like a dance. And a moon-slit
just above the horizon. Truly,

what was once loved is lost in the canyon.

Remember how it got like this,
when desire moved rightly down the oldest streets,

when it was so many beautiful children

pouring their bodies
into the valleys,

where they'll be lost until night itself is an alley of stone.

EVERYTHING WE KNOW

In dream's antechamber beneath the sea,
the river of man's

accumulated knowledge. Capture that river in a jar. Shake.

What you get is a bevy of perspectives. Of clouds,
of the northern ice,

of all words once being one word.

And the air
that begins all thoughts, how did it get here?

The way one brilliant day is tulips/
there are no tulips/there are tulips/all of us are tulips.

We are each breathing a little
of Caesar's dying breath
(we are all breathing a bit of this, molecularly,
it has been proven)—

and like this, in only a matter of time every stone must be life.

A DEEP DARK WOOD

All the raccoon thinks are raccoon thoughts,
and all the chicken thinks are chicken thoughts.
When they think of the thoughts of the other

all they imagine is hunger.
When they think of the thoughts of human beings
all they imagine is hunger.

Raccoons and chickens are very wise, much wiser
than teachers who make nets
from ideas they've stolen from history.

All we eat is grace, and the only way to feel better
about the death of a tomato
is that one day a tomato will feast upon our bones.

For a long time these notions will seem like ideas.
They will be trivia suitable for a game show
or a night in the parlor with your in-laws.

The truth is, it is up to you to love who you are.
When this and all stumbling in the gray forest
become more than ideas, then you are ready.

THE FOURTH DAY

And God said, Let there be lights in the firmament of the heaven to divide the day from the night; and let them be for signs, and for seasons, and for days, and years:

MIGRATION

In the springtime, in the winter, in the fall, there are only

so many seasons to go around.
Soil

scurries along on its regeneration, and whispers

thin in the air
dissipate like the idea of smoke.

Imagine souls intact and strange, like insects,

while years pass like thoughts into a different place.

Few have embodied this so well as you,
you who do not have a name and never will.

What is life? Avoid the easy answers. The clock on the wall

is a suggestion.
Crazed and priceless, what

is laid out as a possibility, faithfully, is what we best do.

LOVE POEM
BEFORE THE END OF TIME

All our lives are crossing the Alps.
It's cold. It's cliff face and sheer drop.

And it's more than possible
a large cat of the wilderness, or a large dog in its pack,
will prepare your pathway for you.

It'll invite you into its mouth, where it's warm.

You may be tempted to go.

If you find a site high up and facing out
you can build a fire and you can see for miles.

The molten core of this planet has made it so. It even
has made oceans,

this and that atom
meeting in a fit of chance.

In another five billion years
the sun, losing energy, and thus expanding, could swallow

this Earth.

INTELLIGENT DESIGN

Knowing the amount of seconds in a lifetime makes little difference to that lifetime. But it does make a difference.

An estimate: if you are thirty years old you have been alive for roughly 946,080,000 seconds. Think about what you've done or could have done with each and every one of them as they receded like vespers from your present.

Or, it's been 15,768,000 minutes, or 262,800 hours, or 10,950 days, and all of these seem like a lot. Or, it has been 30 years, or 3 decades, or 1.5 score, each of these being much more reasonable.

To be modest you could say you've been alive 0.3 centuries, or 0.03 millennia.

If we wanted to get truly serious we could say a thirty year old has been alive for anywhere between 0.00012 and 0.000075 percent of the entire time homo sapiens have been on this earth, depending on your preferred estimate, or roughly 0.00001304 percent of the time the homo genus has walked this planet, or 0.0000005 percent of the time primates have been hanging out, or 0.00000015 percent of the time mammals have wandered the forests and plains and elsewheres of the world.

That all makes you seem pretty small right? And we've hardly begun.

Funny this individual could be under the impression that he or she can understand earth, seeming as this individual has only been alive for 0.00000000659 percent of the time the earth has been around, and even funnier to assume comprehension of this fine universe, having been here for only 0.00000000205 percent of the temporal experience available since the theoretical big bang.

Even under such dire and indicting circumstances we have a tendency to believe ourselves capable of knowing things.

And that would be rather ridiculous, except for the fact that we have indeed been alive for 9,460,800,000,000,000,000,000,000 nanoseconds (that's nine sextillion, four hundred sixty quintillion, eight hundred quadrillion, to be clear), since one nanosecond is to one second as one second is to 31.7 years.

And 9,460,800,000,000,000,000,000 seems like an awful lot.

In fact, it's just about exactly how many meters are in 100 light years, and that, of all things, cannot be a coincidence.

THE LESSON

Solitude provides
many opportunities for correctness, but a heart cannot be
isolated.

There is no removing it from the equation

that equals zero and equals one and does both effortlessly.

To talk with someone, quiet down.

Remain long
after you have been buried
or put to ash and bone.

The moon is thick in the trees, you can sit with it, she is
completely impartial, and listens—

she says, what have you done with the flora with which
you have surrounded yourself, and sustained yourself?

Friend, in the middle of the lake, the oars you've discarded
change nothing.

HOURGLASS

More than anything, sand should not know
when the wave arches its back
like a cat.

It should not pronounce itself glass
and break itself beneath your feet.

Sand should only inhale the sun
as it waits a thousand hours

to steal the blue from the sky, a thousand hours of makeup

blotting each hillside smooth as flour...

I hear time fall forever. I hear it bathe the trees with echoes.
I hear it last or last.

I hear the straps that buckle the shoe to a girl
and her shook-shooking foot.

Hourglass, you are not that sound of water and cardboard

and lifting and circles and barrels and hunger
and diamonds cutting sand, the sand, the sand,

no you are not—

more than anything, time carries its haphazard desire
down your stairs.

More than anything, you should not follow this beach

with yet another.

THE THIRD DAY

And God called the dry land Earth; and the gathering together
of the waters called he Seas: and God saw that it was good.
And God said, Let the earth bring forth grass, the herb
yielding seed, and the fruit tree yielding fruit after his kind,
whose seed is in itself, upon the earth: and it was so.

53

CITRUS

I have shut off the grove, and the light.
For once I allow the night

its effect on every bowing branch.

When I say you are enormous, I mean you are the tree.

On the path, dogs have come
and gone, their tails whipping like emeralds
tossed in the time after money.

The dogs lay beneath the leaves, eating oranges.

The oranges could be you. The oranges could be.

The oranges could be you as a dog
or as a fierce cup of a thousand leaves.

Those thousand leaves watch the night, too.

But today, let's not lie.

Let's fall
into a stark raving madness, like children

whose hands are on fire. We can watch them
fly through the grove,

catching every blade with their dancing fire-hands.

See, when I say dancing
I mean you are the strongest tree for a billion acres.

When I say dancing I mean you are wood.

BEFORE IT'S TOO LATE
I WANTED TO SAY IT'S OKAY

A tree is born: what it was meant to be
it is. Or, *everything happens for a reason*.

These are the things we say to explain the things for which
we don't have
a better explanation.

Or the things we can't bear to allow meaninglessness.

·

In the spring an old woman approaches her end.
Where is she going?

The garden is a gaggle of flowers and the park bench is a place
so she took my hand and led me to the lake.

Fat palms of cloud rose from it
in their languorous way. I tried to see through them

but I couldn't,
and if I could

I would find just air, or the forest
with its billion lives, or Heaven.

Meanwhile, the old woman on her deathbed
composes final letters in her head.

Some end gracefully and some do not.

Some are signed *love* and some *sincerely*. Some *best regards*
and some *from the brink*.

.

The sweep of a skirt
frozen in time.

When we say frozen, what we mean is *does not move*.

Even in photographs, birds seem to rise
above, destined for something more free, or at least a place
closer to the mountaintop.

Put all this together and the sunrise whispers *hurry, hurry*.

It whispers all its explosions, and just because
we can't hear them
doesn't mean they aren't there.

.

Sometimes you have to supply yourself a hammock

in the trees,
or find a cave.

They're the only ways to survive the unknown.

She had taken me by the hand and led me to the lake,
where the herons
with their dignified stares
became statues, and the world

was silent beneath the water: *some end gracefully*
and some do not.

If she shudders
no one will blame her, nor the stone of her cheeks,
nor her flowers,

the impatiens and geraniums

and oceans and oceans and oceans
and oceans and oceans and oceans and oceans of begonias.

All those flowers, without her, still they'll wake.

PREPARING FOR THE FIRE

Even the smallest bits, invisible to the eye, belong
to us and we to them. Rain is the same.

Leaving this place is hope for a red morning.
A moth pounds the window, in love with human light.

I walk through the front door, and you say
One day you will wake to find yourself finished.

I walk through the front door. Look at the time,
you say. Look at the time.

Your bags and my thousand flaming trees are full.
Hills fall over each other, rumpling their outfits.

In the ghosts between clothes and skin, so much.
So much, while our cold forest warms itself with itself.

THE AFTERLIFE

All the imagination you've exhausted on the thought

that those in heaven are not ghosts

has brought you no closer to understanding.

Ghosts are only here,
on earth, as heaven
is for those who have wandered
around their suffering

and have seen through it, like those who left earth

excommunicated or saved

but blessed either way.

That's what they say. The earth is for seeds and trees
and Heaven is

for those who believe
I'm leaving, I'm leaving

the freedom that comes from confinement,

and what that means
for the soul—

the soul—

that thing or no-thing which may or may not
be

now, or ever.

THE GUN

Soul may be the most damaged word,

to watch the tree bloom
and return to earth…

                         a sense of humor, the scent of ash

and the sobbing of wolves…

flower petals
stand on end and seem to gallop in the wind.

They cross the sidewalk, they cross
the long grasses and fallow plains, they fold into the evening
to smell the carbon
from which we all are made.

        I'm sorry if my hands are a little cold.
        I'm sorry if this is the way of the world.
        You have very shiny eyes, it's true, they are

like two dimes under the sun.

Carbon, we can tell the ages of fossils and moons by it,

and of our hands,
but not of our thoughts.

.

We did not need water, we did not need water,
we *were* water, and though

    fate is a star you cannot place

on your astronomical charts, it burns brightly, it has lived
billions of years
and has billions left to live. Eventually

you could learn its secrets, which of its chemicals
commingle at the ball

draped in fine fabrics and jewelry and all the propriety
of science.

And that learning will, like carbon, like water, become need.

.

Go on, go on ahead of me, let the sand go on
for miles. It'll always be a beach, even one grain.

Go on complaining against the automobiles. We are each
the street

taking care of its family. We are asphalt.

In the summer a child will wonder
why our surface appears
watery, though it is not. To think, a miracle in the real
world:

the miracle is the time before and after the miracle.

So let's not worry
about forever—

that's a long time from now.

•

SO:

A black fog,

a black fog you run through,

a black fog you run through, and run through,

past the church, past the post office, past convenience store
and firehouse, past the cemetery, down the winding road,
through the hairpin turn, past the pale trailers whose tire
swings cradle boys yet to know girls, past the anonymous
houses, brick houses and mobile homes and houses on stilts,
until you see the schoolyard, you see the openness that is the
way to the big river, you see the steel mill with its blood
orange metal, you know you could enter the highway and
continue running, past the burnt out hole of the city, past the
paper factory now only an idea, removed like ambition save
for its single smokestack and the stories about it, and the
river, along the river, the original thoughts, from the very
beginning, when shouting and listening were different only to
those far away—

    you can follow the route of all heroes to a new home—

you can smash a spider with a shoe, or make
the tender deadbolt align ecstatically—

you can do this and say *there is no need for fear*
in the purple of the night, when a man outside, nearby,

cocks a gun.

dear angel...

THE SECOND DAY

And God made the firmament, and divided the waters which were under the firmament from the waters which were above the firmament: and it was so. And God called the firmament Heaven. And the evening and the morning were the second day.

THE BIG BANG

I.

In a box I held up a thousand little hells

and in each I found memory and her friends
and a slew of numbers
saying they were the one true language

and in their conceit
I thought, this, a *day*, is not a fraction I have to recognize.

Nor are minute nor hour nor second nor week
nor the other products of separation.

In the absence of these I saw so much care
and I saw your hands in the air

and a finch making its sound from inside of joy.

Time is new. Now, new time is new. Now,
new time new, again,
new, now, new, again.

71

Each time we say it
it becomes,

and the subject of us becomes the object we watch.

It is as if we are viewing ourselves from very far away.

•

On yet another fanatical night

we've broken the day into shapes

of survival. This is pure happiness or endless vigil

just like the candle
whose wax is running out

is a metaphor for us, for our body, our being, yet our wax
will never run out.

During every red minute

what we thought we thought
changes to irrelevance and so too does what we were.

Meanwhile, a mudslide in South America swallows dozens,

and in Brooklyn
an Ecuadorian is unknowingly

dragged twenty miles
by a delivery van. And what of the meanings of their lives

except that this may be
their most notable moment?

●

Never would I want the moon

to stop its stay in the sky—not when the sun clatters
against its shadow,
not when the autumn light cuts its smallness into halves.

When the enlightened sage encountered his old friend

after so many years,

his old friend
considered him a fool.

It's good to remember this when we listen, or when
we do not.

•

Above buildings, birds
hang in the air like bullets

on film. The terrible winter beneath the streetlights
staggers on its slow path, and when I want it gone

it's unclear whether that thought
is the proper thought to have—

sometimes grace

is the first sip of water
after six days' trek through the desert.

In the end, no one can kiss this life
too long, not even when its love is far too large to swallow.

2.

Even after I died, I could not close my eyes
as the tiny empires

piled up their bodies.

Four quarters for a dollar, the playground leaves

make small tornadoes of possibility, and at the waterfront

the poor are music as they wash
their pants. Their song and the wind, their song
and the wind.

At the waterfront, a ship comes in and on its side
in stenciled block letters
is the word for our understanding; seven black-faced laughing
gulls call out

the ship's name in staccato, and it's true

the water is cast-iron deep and the groan it makes
sounds like what it is: children.

Even after I died I could not close my eyes, not even

after I died.

.

The egret, sculpture of the wilderness, its legs
like flagpoles and atop them
this pale flag, this body of the bird, with its flickering
heart and long throat.

When the bird leaves earth, I plan to live
with the contentment
of an egg

for fourteen billion years. When the egg cracks or is cracked
there is life
or there is not life or there is, but either way

it will return to the soil. There a tree will grow or grass
for the walking on of animals and people.

In this universe, this place that was once just one tiny hot ball

of possibility
before its billowing out into the everything
we are,

not a place do we step is not a home:

egret, even you

with your deliberate beak, where you presently rest
someone has been born.

3.

All these years that have passed

since the beginning, and still, as April's branches rush
to the earth,

Heaven is not a possibility
we can reject.

Is this mine? Is the light data as well? Everything everyone

hears
is wheat

as ideas are added to the fire. This wood provides the fire—

like the clouds, a crowd gathers
to watch the flames, the forest a pet held too tightly...

•

The house I'm going to fill is full of air.

It has several rooms and in them
will be many tables, as there have long been many tables

though in eternity there are none.

In this room
rain is everywhere and insects cannot find their way.

And these minor works of art that befall us, that ask us
to trace black lines of distinction
between the great and the truly great—

I have to ask the animal with his terrific antlers
what he thinks of these,

whether time would seek truth, if only
it had desires.

Look around you, he says, *look into the field.*
Look and see
the pendulum, see it swinging back…

But the bodies here are not so like the stars.
And if somehow

I wrong this life, may I suffer

so, so many ages. For all that has been created, beautiful
or not,
is juvenilia.

4.

There will be losses, the crashing of skin against skin.
Or when two forests grow into one forest.

One might, on an evening of bare knees, expect time
to birth a novel,

cold and uncompromising, each letter
unchangeable

behind its mask of paper. And that novel

could be a darling
counting barges

as they pour their enormous stomachs across the river.

I'm sure the prayer works. It moves each brittle hour
through an ocean

of mornings, when the orange shepherd

drives the seed from its bed. The seed reaches up, up, long
past siesta

while this hard pack of days rattles in its chambers.

One might expect
time to do any number of things, and that, too, is just the way

with this happy fate, pulling us toward its realization...

•

Deep red tongue of sky, ambush
of concrete onto this pound of earth, ongoing threat
of the Truth

waking as you sleep to say

you should never have tried to find me.

What is happiness? This is what is

that cannot be changed, this war of togetherness, this
countdown

not to the mortality of after-life,
but to the mortality of before-life...

accept it and death's pleasantry

so humanity can chandelier its beauty for each green plant
to suck light into.

•

And, finally, a lamp which holds down a corner
with its coat of amber,

the city and its magnificent manger,
the *origin* of possibilities and more errors
than you can count—

a traveler
pauses

in the middle of a bridge
to gather her breath.

She stands there in the middle

and she can look to her left
or to her right, and she can look up or down.

But all this looking is only that, because on this bridge

the middle is where she is, and this is a very long bridge:

when it comes time to end, no worries.
When it comes time to end, no worries, no worries.

When it comes time to begin, no worries.
When it comes time to begin, no worries, no worries, no worries.

THE FIRST DAY

In the beginning God created the heaven and the earth. And the earth was without form, and void; and darkness was upon the face of the deep. And the Spirit of God moved upon the face of the waters. And God said, Let there be light: and there was light.

NOTE

The retroactive chronological predictions of the Genesis 1 model of existence are largely mirrored by reality, yet there are some compelling incongruities with the carbon dating and physical model evidence favored by the scientifically minded. As an illustration of the latter approach, Carl Sagan popularized a curiosity in which the entire existence of the universe is plotted as if its nearly 14 billion years were just 1 year, a sort of temporal 13,820,000,000:1 scale model. Using this method, the "cosmic calendar" would shake out in roughly the following manner:

January 1st Big Bang
September 1st Formation of the Sun, with Planets Following
December 18th First Fish
December 20th First Land Plants
December 23rd First Reptiles
December 30th Dinosaurs Extinct
December 31st
    ~10:24 p.m. First Primitive Humans
    11:44 p.m. Domestication of Fire
    11:59:47 p.m. Invention of Writing ("History" Begins)
    11:59:54-56 p.m. Births of Buddha, Jesus, Muhammad
    11:59:59 p.m. Emergence of the Scientific Method
Midnight: *Now*, the minute you are reading this

Most compelling here is not just the fact that more than two-thirds of the universe's lifespan has not included the planet Earth, let alone humans, which made their belated appearance well after children's bedtime on the year's last day, but that

fish actually make their debut before fruit-bearing trees—
millions of years before, in fact. The Genesis model,
simplified below, would find this somewhat counterintuitive
fact displeasing:

Day 1—earth and light
Day 2—the heavens
Day 3—trees and fruit
Day 4—stars and time
Day 5—fish and birds
Day 6—people and animals
Day 7—rest and blessing

As you can see, Genesis, a document historically attributed to
Moses as the first of the five Mosaic texts composing the
Pentateuch (Torah), and one composed sometime between
2500 and 3000 years ago, has trees coming first, then fish not
the next day, but the day after that.

Interestingly, the seven days described in Genesis 1:1-2:3,
and discussed in the book you are holding, are from one
source, while the often Romanticized and popularized Adam
and Eve creation myth, from Genesis 2:4-24, is from a wholly
different source. There is much speculation as to how these
logistically incompatible stories (in the first story, male and
female are created at the same time; in the second, female
comes from the rib of the male; in the first, animal appears
before man; in the second, man—but not woman—before
animal) came to be together, but together they are.

Regardless of specifics, it is through and in beauty that they,
and science, and the glorious and routine mythology of every
day, lend us and our lives the light of meaning.

ACKNOWLEDGMENTS

Many, many thanks to the journals who have published poems from this collection, many with different form or title:

Beloit Poetry Journal (excerpt from "The Big Bang")
Boston Review ("Politic")
Borderlands ("Near-Death Experience")
Cincinnati Review ("Hourglass")
Connecticut Review ("The Circuit")
Copper Nickel ("The Lesson," excerpts from "The Big Bang")
Diode ("The Youth" and "Travelogue")
Escape Into Life ("A Deep Dark Wood," "Intelligent Design," "The Afterlife," and "The Gun")
Flyway ("Everything We Know")
Kenyon Review Online ("Citrus")
The Laurel Review ("A Brief Essay on Sameness" and "The Nightly News")
Ninth Letter ("Preparing for the Fire")
Passages North ("Tyrannosaurus")
Quarterly West ("The Human Experience")
Parcel (excerpts from "The Big Bang")
Permafrost ("Holiday")
Route 7 Review ("Lost on the Planet Earth" and "Migration")
Salamander (excerpts from "The Big Bang," "Before It's Too Late I Wanted to Say It's Okay")
Sentence ("Parable")
The Southern Review ("Meditation on the Bear Finding Himself" and "The Deep")
Thrush Poetry Journal ("Love Poem Before the End of Time" and "Sonnet for the Airborne")

The Toronto Quarterly (excerpt from "The Big Bang")
Verse Daily (reissues of an excerpt from "The Big Bang," "The
    Human Experience")

And lastly, the following poem appeared in the chapbook
Elegy for the Builder's Wife, published by Blue Hour Press:
"Preparing for the Fire."

I'd also like to thank Andrew Neuendorf and Trey Moody for
helping me name this book.

ABOUT GOLD WAKE PRESS

Gold Wake Press, an independent publisher, was founded in Boston, Massachusetts in 2008 by J. Michael Wahlgren. All Gold Wake Press titles are available at amazon.com, barnesandnoble.com, spdbooks.org, and via order from your local bookstore.

Recent & Forthcoming Titles:

Andy Briseño's *Down and Out*
Talia Bloch's *Inheritance*
Sarah Strickley's *Fall Together*
Eileen G'Sell's *Life After Rugby*
Erin Stalcup's *Every Living Species*
Glenn Shaheen's *Carnivalia*
Frances Cannon's *The High and Lows of Shapeshift Ma and Big-Little Frank*
Justin Bigos' *Mad River*
Kelly Magee's *The Neighborhood*
Kyle Flak's *I Am Sorry for Everything in the Whole Entire Universe*
David Wojciechowski's *Dreams I Never Told You & Letters I Never Sent*
Keith Montesano's *Housefire Elegies*
Mary Quade's *Local Extinctions*
Adam Crittenden's *Blood Eagle*
Lesley Jenike's *Holy Island*
Hannah Stephenson's *In the Kettle, the Shriek*

ABOUT THE AUTHOR

Nick Courtright is also the author of *Punchline*, a National Poetry Series finalist published in 2012 by Gold Wake Press. His work has appeared in journals such as *Harvard Review*, *The Southern Review*, *Boston Review*, and *Kenyon Review Online*, among many others, and a chapbook, *Elegy for the Builder's Wife*, is available from Blue Hour Press. He lives in Austin, Texas.

Feel free to find him at nickcourtright.com.

fiat lux

CPSIA information can be obtained
at www.ICGtesting.com
Printed in the USA
FFOW02n0314300518
46855720-49065FF